FOLLOWING GOD IS EASY

SO WHY DO WE MAKE IT SO HARD?

Vern Kaska III

Published in the United States of America by

Spirit Media and our logos are trademarks of
Spirit Media Inc
205 S Academy Street #3251
Cary, NC 27519
1 (888) 800-3744 | https://spiritmedia.us

Religion & Spirituality | Christian Living | Spiritual Growth

Paperback ISBN: 979-8-89307-236-5
eBook ISBN: 979-8-89307-235-8
PDF ISBN: 979-8-89307-234-1
Library of Congress Control Number: 2026907224

Table of Contents

Opening

Following God is Easy. All you have to do is give all areas of your life over to Him, trust in Him, and if you do this, you will have a peaceful, blessed life and live eternally in Heaven...

Wouldn't it be nice if it were that easy? If we could just read the sentence above and have our minds immediately grasp it? If we could instantliy give all our fears, cares, worries, and anxieties to Him and feel everlasting peace within ourselves? If that were the case, there would be no reason for me to write this book or for you continue to reading it. But unfortunately, it is not that easy.

Our minds sometimes need more explanation, and the points need to be explained repeatedly. That is what I am going to try to accomplish with this book, but as you read it, I want the opening statement, "Following God is Easy," to always remain at the forefront of your mind because it *is* that simple.

If you are reading this book, it is because it is God's plan for you to do so. You did not find this book by mistake. It does not matter if you have followed God your whole life and know every verse of the Bible, or if you are a person who has committed every sin possible and thinks there is no way that God could forgive you. This book will hopefully offer direction to help you grow in your relationship with the Lord. My prayer is that the Holy Spirit moves within you as you read this book.

ONE

How it All Started

L et me start with a confession: I'm not a pastor, theologian, or seminary graduate. I'm someone who reads the Bible daily, prays regularly, and still struggles—just like you probably do. So why am I writing this book? Because I believe God asked me to, and I've learned that obedience matters more than credentials.

As a person, I am not qualified to write this book, but as a vessel for the Holy Spirit, we are able to do all things through Christ. My prayer for this book is that none of the concepts or ideas are mine, but that God uses my hands to type in a meaningful direction that will help you grow in your faith and in your relationship with God.

I am writing this book because I believe God has called me to do so. He has given me ideas and concepts that I think will help people in their walk with God.

It all started for me about four years ago. I watched a movie that looked like it had the potential to be great, but when it was over I was very disappointed, and I started to realize that all movies are exactly the same. There are never any new ideas or original plots anymore. I went to bed that night saying to myself, I wish I could write because I know that I could come up with a way better plot and a new, original story better than what I just watched.

The reason I said that I wished I could write is because I am horrible at it. I can barely spell the word: "cat." Typing out a long e-mail at work, something that would take most people five minutes, would take me thirty. There are always tons of misspelled words, and when I go back and read the sentences I wrote, they would not make any sense at all, or the sentence meaning would not be what I was trying to portray. So, the thought of me writing a whole book just seemed like it would be impossible.

The problem was that same night, I already started coming up with a new plot for a book. The first and last chapter came to me within minutes. I had whole conversations in my head, and the last chapter of the book seemed as though it would write itself. That next weekend, my wife and son went to visit friends in another state, and because of work commitments, I could not join them.

I had the weekend to myself. I decided to just try and write the first chapter of the book. It was like I thought. I got about one paragraph in, and my whole screen was full of red and blue lines with all the misspelled words and sentence structure errors. I went back and fixed all the errors in the first paragraph and looked at the clock and one hour had already passed.

Then I decided I would fix all the errors as I was typing, but as I tried that I would lose my train of thought on what I was trying to write. This turned out to be exactly like I expected.

Finally, for one last-ditch effort, I decided I would not care about the errors. I was just going to type out the whole chapter and fix everything at the end. To my surprise, this worked. It still took me about three more hours to write the first chapter but once I started typing it was just like the first night, the story seemed to start writing itself.

After I finished the first chapter that day, it was about two weeks before I tried to write again. I am in information technology (IT), and I travel for work so I decided that rather than watching movies on all my plane flights, I could use that time and the downtime in my hotels to write my book.

It took me about two years of writing during my travels to complete my book, but I finally completed it. Then I hired a self-publishing company to edit and help publish my book which took about another three months.

My book *The Spy Who Did Not Know* has been out for about two years now. I paid the publishing company $1,549.00 to help me edit and publish the book. So far, during these two years, it has sold about forty-six copies, earning me around $170. I did have grand thoughts that my first book might be an instant bestseller, but I now know that God gave me the ideas and passion to author that book just to show me that I could write a book.

I also made the mistake of writing the first book to fit a worldview. It has language and subject matter that, looking back, could have been written differently. A few years ago, God planted a seed—an urge to write that wouldn't go away. My first book showed me that the process was possible. This is why that process mattered.

I am not sure if there is any way I would have believed, or started trying to author this book, if not for that one. It was around the time I was writing the fifth chapter of my old book that God started laying on my heart to author this book. I almost stopped writing that one to start this one, but at this point, I was not sure if I would be able to get it published. I had already put a lot of time and effort into it, so I decided to finish it, but I still struggled with this decision. If God's plan were for this book and He just used the first one to get me started, why would I delay? It was weighing on me, but I decided that I had to finish the process. I needed to figure out the entire process of publishing a book to see if I really could do it.

This is one of the premises behind this book and why following God can sometimes feel so difficult. What is the right answer? If God tells you to do something, should you stop everything and do it? The answer is yes. On the other hand, if the process is delayed and it takes more time than you think it should, then that may also be God's plan. If He is never wrong, then this book will be published at exactly the right time. So why should I have anxiety and worry about what to do when either way is fine? The answer is I should not worry.

All I can do is keep praying over the process and trust it will all turn out okay. If I let worry and fear get in the way, then I will find excuses not to write the book at all, and that would cause me to be more worried, because I am not doing what God asked me to do. The back and forth will never end, so the best way to manage that is to not worry in the first place, but to just let the Lord lead you and be at peace with yourself.

While reading this book, please be open-minded; if there is something you disagree with, just move on and continue to read. Do not let evil put thoughts in your mind or get fixated on one point that will distract you from reading all the other good points in the book that will help you grow in your relationship with God.

A common point I will be making in this book is how evil will use contradictions to keep your mind on things that are not important and distract you from the things that matter. So please, the first time you read through this book do not let yourself be distracted by ideas or points you disagree with. Just focus on the new ideas and points that will help you grow in your relationship with God.

Then, if you feel the need to, when you are done you can go back and disagree with all the ideas you do not like. But hopefully after reading this book, you will no longer have the desire to fight the little things that evil tries to distract us with and you will only be focused on a relationship with God.

Reflection

Are there things God has been calling you to do that you have been ignoring?

Two

Why am I Reading this Book?

A big theme in this book will be about spending time with God and growing your relationship with Him. So, it seems like that is the way we should start. I would like you to ask yourself what you are looking to get out of this book, or, if you are in a place where you are comfortable with prayer, pray to God and ask Him to use this book to grow your faith.

I believe that everyone, from preachers to non-believers, will be able to use this book to grow in a relationship with the Lord, but I think it is a good exercise to start asking questions about why we feel we are not fully there yet. Not that I think we can ever become perfect, but I think it would be good to start thinking about the ways we need to grow and the things that are holding us back. Everyone's walk with the Lord is going to be different, so now is a good time to start reflecting on where you are in your walk and where you would like to end up.

I would like to start the process of reading this book not as a knowledge transfer of information from me to you, but as a process where you begin trying to bring God into every aspect of your life, even through the process of reading this book. As you read all the words in this book, have an openness to the Holy Spirit to see if they pertain to you. Don't just read them but open that relationship with God to see if they truly apply to you or not.

If no questions come to mind, what are some questions you can ask yourself? If you are a non-believer, then the question might be, what is holding me back? Unfortunately, a lot of times this answer is because of other believers. Or maybe you've had bad experiences with people in the church, maybe even a bad experience with the pastor of a church. If that's been your experience, I understand why you might hesitate.

But here's what I've learned: the behavior of other people—even people who claim to follow Christ—has nothing to do with whether God is real or whether He loves you. Your relationship with God is between you and Him alone. No one else gets a vote. It does not matter how anyone else treats you or acts, because while we are all called to be disciples of God, only you can make the decision to accept or reject God. So, if that is the decision you are trying to make, the only two that can influence that decision are you and God. Other people's actions should not have an influence on this decision at all. If you limit the decision-making for your salvation to only you and the Holy Trinity, once you feel the love of God, then your decision will become an easy one to make.

Another question you may be asking yourself is, how far do I really want to take this relationship with God? One holdback of non-believers may be that there is no way that they could ever be as good or devoted as others they see worshiping God. Well, the good thing about this is that it is not a competition, and good works do not get you into Heaven. Only accepting Jesus as your Lord and Savior does. From there, the rest is about your relationship with God, and the only way to have that relationship is to start it and see where it goes. Again, the only ones that should have a say in your salvation are you and God.

The question for believers is where am I truly in my walk with God? Am I a Christian who only goes to church on Sundays and does my own things the rest of the week? If I am, why is that? What are the things of this world that are holding me back from spending more time with God? If you are a true believer and have accepted your salvation, then you have felt the peace and love of God. That peace and love are unlike anything else on this earth. So, what is stopping me from chasing that feeling every moment I have the opportunity to chase it? Or what is stopping me from growing my relationship with the Lord?

If you are a believer who spends daily time in prayer and in the Bible then you have probably already come up with a question for yourself, or you already know what you want to get out of this book and we both know that God led you to this book for some reason. I just pray that reason helps you grow in your walk with the Lord.

Whatever your questions are, I would encourage you to keep them in the back of your mind while reading this book, while at the same time bringing them to God in prayer. One of the most important things in life, and the principle of this book, is constantly working on your relationship with God.

When Jesus was asked which is the greatest commandment in the law, He answered: *"Love the Lord your God with all your heart and with all your soul and with all your mind" (Matthew 22:37 NIV).* That, above all things, is what we are asked to do.

How then can you love God with all your heart if you do not have a relationship with Him? Think about the people you are closest to and have the most meaningful relationships with. They are probably the people you spend most of your time with. It would be hard to have a meaningful relationship with someone you only talked to once a year. The same is true with your relationship with the Lord, which needs lots of time to grow meaningfully.

Reflection

Why am I reading this book?

THREE

Contradiction

Early in this book, I would like to address something evil uses often to confuse us: contradiction, or what our minds perceive as contradiction. The dictionary definition is:

con·tra·dic·tion

/ˌkäntrəˈdikSH(ə)n/

noun

noun: **contradiction**; plural noun: **contradictions**

A combination of statements, ideas, or features of a situation that are opposed to one another.

"The proposed new system suffers from a set of internal contradictions"

- A person, thing, or situation in which <u>inconsistent</u> elements are present.

  "the paradox of using force to overcome force is a real contradiction"

- The statement of a position opposite to one already made.

  "the second sentence appears to be in flat contradiction of the first"

I am sure most people reading this book know what the word contradiction means, so you are probably wondering why I felt the need to write out the whole definition for you to read before proceeding with this chapter.

The first reason is that most of the time we just read words and then move on to the next one and if this chapter is going to be about just one word, then I think it is important that we actually spend time making sure that we realize the true and full meaning of the word.

The second is that I like the way the two different interpretations show the difference between a real contradiction–"using force to overcome force"—and an apparent, or what I like to call a perceived contradiction "the second sentence appears to be in flat contradiction of the first." So, is the second sentence a contradiction of the first, or are we just perceiving it to be?

When it comes to studying religion or growing in our faith, the easiest thing evil can do to slow down our progress is to give us a contradiction. You think you have everything figured out, and then you hear that small voice saying, "But wait a minute what about this? There is no way that can be true if this is true." If you find yourself always listening to that voice, you will always find an excuse why things are not good, or God is not real… Or you may become so frustrated thinking about it that you no longer want to continue. My point is we need to make sure we do not get consumed with unimportant things that do not matter, and instead try to stay focused on the bigger picture, our relationship with God.

On the other hand, sometimes we do need to listen to that small voice that says, "But wait a minute, what about this." There is always a voice in every decision. I know this in itself is a contradiction, but that voice can be both a good thing and a bad thing. It all depends on how you listen to that voice. Are you listening to that voice from a place of acceptance in trying to grow with the Lord or are you fighting as hard as you can to live life the way you want to live it?

This again will go back to the point where it is very easy for the contradictions to become so overwhelming that you just give up and that is why I would like to start early in this book pointing out how easy it is for evil to use this trick to slow down your spiritual life.

So, what are some of the big perceived contradictions that believers face that hold us back? The biggest one is the one we hear in almost every sermon that is preached: the message that starts by telling you that all you need to do is say a simple prayer accepting Jesus into your heart as your Lord and Savior. Once you do that, you will be saved, and you can never lose your salvation. Then, in the very next message, you hear someone asking whether you are really doing enough and living out your life for Jesus. So, which is it? Can I just say a prayer and be done, or do I have to become a disciple and spend all the days of my life living for Jesus? How do we know if we are doing too much or not enough? Are we doing what is right in God's eyes, or are we being deceived by evil? How do we know if we are truly saved, and can we lose our salvation?

I would say that once you have your salvation, no, you can never lose it, but if you just say the prayer and keep living life the way the world and non-believers do, then the question does have to be asked whether you were ever really saved in the first place. If you truly meant the prayer of salvation, then you should start to feel the conviction to live life and love according to the teaching of Jesus. If you do not feel this conviction, are you sure you really meant the salvation prayer at all? The only way to answer that is through spending time with the Holy Trinity and reading the teachings of Jesus in the Bible. A good Bible passage for this is (John 15:1-4 NIV):

> *I am the true vine, and my Father is the gardener. He cuts off every branch in me that bears no fruit, while every branch that does bear fruit He prunes so that it will be even more fruitful. You are already clean because of the word I have spoken to you. Remain in me, as I also remain in you. No branch can bear fruit by itself; it must remain in the vine. Neither can you bear fruit unless you remain in me.*

From the verse, we can conclude that we must remain in Jesus and while we do need to have that moment when we first accept Christ, it is also clear that we must also remain in Him. I can try to explain this perceived contradiction to you, but only you can choose how you receive that explanation. You can either get hung up on the technical aspects and spend more time trying to answer the question than spending time with God, or you can take the questions to God and grow that relationship with Him.

This is also how you can answer the question for yourself, about whether you are doing enough as a Christian. If God is calling you to go out and spread the good news, then go do it and you will find peace. If He has not put that desire in your heart yet, that is okay. Just spend as much time with the Holy Trinity as you can to find what God wants from you. That way you can discover peace in your life, and you will not feel guilty about anything.

Spending time growing your relationship is more important than figuring out all the mysteries of the universe. It may be that you are just not meant to know the answer to that question right now, but as you grow more in your relationship with God, the answers you are looking for will be revealed to you.

The one thing I can tell you is that all God is looking for from you is a relationship and your love. If you ever think you find a contradiction to that point, you can know for sure that it is from evil; be careful not to listen to that voice.

I am trying to use this chapter to show how easy it is for evil to use contradiction to slow us down in our relationships with God. But once we start to realize this, we can start to use this to our advantage. God never contradicts Himself. Every word in the Bible is perfect and precisely placed. Since the completion of the Bible people have been trying to find contradictions or ways to disprove the Bible, and none have been able to do it.

Not one person in over 2000 years has been able to disprove one word of the Bible. For millennia, the Bible has endured scrutiny and criticism, yet it continues to transform lives. Its truths have proven resilient, not because scholars can't debate its details, but because its core message—that God loves us and wants a relationship with us—remains unchanging and verifiable in the lives of believers. This should prove God's involvement in its writing and show that God is real. Especially considering that the Bible contains approximately 2,500 prophecies, of which over 2,000 have been fulfilled exactly as written.

I know some of you may be getting that small voice in your head that wants to disagree with me, saying that not every word of the Bible and every story in the Bible is true. But that is why different religions and people for 2,000 years have been trying to find just one word that is not correct. Because either the Bible is 100% true and accurate or it is 100% false. It cannot be somewhere in between.

We have a God who created insects to pollinate flowers, the moon that control the tides of the earth, processes like photosynthesis, and complex cells in our bodies, all the way down to something so small as the atom. He made all the things in this universe that are so complex that we still do not, nor probably ever will understand them. So, to think that God, who created the universe in all its complexity, would make a mistake with even one word of the Bible, is absurd. That is why I say that the Bible must be 100 % accurate or 100% false. If you ever find anything that contradicts the Bible, you can rest assured that the interpretation is wrong, not the Bible.

Now that we know God does not use contradictions, when you see them in your faith, you can just ignore the contradiction and move on without wasting your time on it. If you cannot find proof of it in the Bible, then you need to be genuinely concerned with that information.

That makes it easy to exclude ideas that are not in the Bible, but what about all the controversy that different religions make from the same Bible? There are whole denominations that were created over different interpretations of different verses in the Bible. This again is where you need to have your relationship with God and pray about how you are using the information you are learning from the Bible.

One thing I will caution you to do is to make sure you know the full context behind the verse. I think a lot of people take just one sentence and use it to make it fit their agenda or the outcome they want most. This can be dangerous and probably another contradiction that evil will use.

In the paragraph above I tell you not to use one verse of the Bible to draw conclusions, but there is also a possible contradiction to this. The Bible is a living document. The words are as relevant today as they were 2,000 years ago, and there are no accidents when it comes to God. If you have prayed to God for answers and then you find yourself reading the Bible and the verse sounds like an answer to your question, then it most likely is. This is why it is so important to have prayer time and time spent in God's Word.

It is called God's Word for a reason, and sometimes that reason is to answer your questions or speak to you directly. This is another reason you can conclude the Bible is from God. Who else could place a Bible verse in front of you at the exact moment and time that you need to hear it? God may not come out and give you an audible voice to let you know He is there, but if you invest the time and effort in Him, there will be no doubt in your mind when He is speaking to you.

Reflection

Are there any contradictions in your life holding you back from a relationship with God?

FOUR

Free Will

This chapter is about free will, the best and worst thing God gave to humankind. I say it is the worst thing God gave us because wouldn't it be wonderful if there was no way for us to sin and disappoint God? I personally would love it if my mind or body was not capable of doing wrong or committing sin. Life would be so much easier. We would not need any law enforcement or any man-made laws at all. Adam and Eve would never have been capable of eating from the tree of the knowledge of good and evil, and we would all still be in the Garden of Eden. It sounds perfect, and I am one of the few people who would like to live life that way. Some would probably say that we are not living our own lives without free will. If you have no free will to make your own choices, then every day of your life would be very predictable and probably get boring. Also, our relationship with God would be boring for Him. I am not going to claim to know how time works for God, because we know that He knows everything, every outcome, and has control over every situation. But because of free will, I believe the choices we make still matter to Him in the moment we make them. That is what makes every one of our relationships unique and special to God. Free will is the only way we could truly choose God. And it is what allows every one of us to have a different relationship with God.

We are created beings who were created to have a relationship with God, yet He still gave us the free will to choose whether to have that relationship at all. It seems like a no-brainer how you should use your free will when you look at it from a high level. Let's break it down to a simple conversation.

God breathes life into Us: "Thanks, God, for creating me. What do I owe you in return?"

God: "Just spend time with me and tell others about how great that time with me is."

Us: "Wow that sounds easy, but it looks like there are a lot of fun things to do with this life. What if I just want to do my own thing and get too busy to spend time with you?"

God: "That is okay I will be here when you get done but just be aware that I created you to be with me so you will never be fully fulfilled or at peace as long as you are apart from me."

Us: "Okay but it is my choice, right? I mean I know you are busy, so do you really have time for me anyway."

God: "Yes, it is your choice, and I have created eternity to make sure I have time for just you, so please make time for me."

Following God is easy. So why do we make it so hard?

Eternity is a concept that I think most of us cannot fully understand. Consider this: roughly 117 billion humans have ever lived. If God spent the equivalent of every person's lifetime in relationship with them, that would be trillions of years—yet against eternity, that's essentially zero percent of His time. God created eternity partly to ensure He would always have time for you. The question isn't whether God has time for you. It's whether you'll make time for Him.

One other point that needs to be mentioned when it comes to eternity—and why it is so important for you to use your free will to know Jesus died on the cross for you and to have that personal relationship with God—is that we are going to spend eternity somewhere.

We are created as eternal beings, not temporary creations. If our existence ends with death, then what we do in life is irrelevant. If you ever wondered about the purpose of life, it is to have a relationship with God and to get to Heaven. That way you can spend eternity with the Holy Trinity in Heaven.

One hundred years is considered a long life, but if you look at the numbers above, it is no time at all. In some ways, it may not seem fair that God only gives us 100 years to figure out how wonderful his love and grace are. But on the other hand, He is only asking for 100 years to obey His word to get to Heaven for eternity. He doesn't even ask for a full 100 years. He just asks for the last ones to be spent with Him. He could ask for one million years of faith to make sure you are truly worthy to enter Heaven's gates, but no, He only asks for one prayer— one moment in time confessing Jesus as your Lord and Savior and accepting Him into your heart. Then after that moment, all He asks for is a relationship with you. He made it so simple for us, yet most of us make following God very complicated and tend to overthink it until it becomes too much to deal with.

So, if God has a plan for everything and already knows everything that has and will happen then how can we say we truly have free will? I think the best way to explain this is like watching a rerun of an old football game. You already know who wins and who loses. You know which part of the game not to get excited about because you know nothing big will come out of the next play and you know all the big plays that will happen because you have already seen the game before. But the first time you watched the game it was more exciting. You did not know the outcome or how the drives would end so for every play you still had hope for either a turnover or a touchdown depending on who you were rooting for.

Now for God, I think it is like watching both games at the same time. He is excited to see what decisions you are going to make while already knowing what they are. But unlike you watching a rerun of the old game I think God is able to put multiple games together to get His desired outcome.

I believe you are here at this specific moment in time and in this place because it is your best chance to make the right decisions to have a relationship with God to get to Heaven and to spend eternity with Him. Or it could be that you are here at this time on earth because at this time you have the greatest potential to help others make the right decisions to have that relationship with God.

Your question might be: If God has rearranged all of space and time for us to be here because it is our best chance at Heaven, then how are there people out there suffering endlessly with no hope that will not make it to Heaven?

I do not think God puts people on this earth who are destined to go to hell. But again, they may be on this earth because it was their time to help others get to Heaven. Sometimes seeing the destruction of others makes us not want to go through that ourselves. Seeing that person suffering may help others turn their own life around. The scripture verse that best describes this is (John 9:1-5 NIV):

As He went along, He saw a man blind from birth. His disciples asked Him, "Rabbi, who sinned, this man or his parents, that he was born blind?"

"Neither this man nor his parents sinned," said Jesus, "but this happened so that the works of God might be displayed in him. As long as it is day, we must do the works of Him who sent me. Night is coming, when no one can work. While I am in the world, I am the light of the world."

This is why we should live like Jesus and love everyone, because we do not know God's plan. You never know how many people have been pushed to God by witnessing the actions of sinful people.

I know it does not seem fair that God can use some people's tragedies to lead others to Heaven, but I think we still must remember that it was their own free will to be this way. He did not ask them to make the choices they made, but if some good can come out of their bad choices, then maybe it is better they were here at this time than never being here at all.

But don't let their bad choices be in vain. Learn the lesson for yourself from their failures without having to go through them. We all know people who have stories of how they had to hit rock bottom before they could find Jesus. Jesus will be with you wherever you are, so don't wait until you hit rock bottom before you find Him. Find Him first on your own before you reach the bottom. That way you will not have to hit the bottom at all.

I realize from my Bible verse above that the blind man did not make a choice to be blind. I am kind of grouping two different scenarios together. But the overall point is if it is the will of God, then it must be for good.

Reflection

How have you used your free will so far in your life and how would you like to use it going forward?

____

____

____

____

____

____

____

____

____

____

____

____

____

FIVE

Suffering

What follows isn't doctrine—it's what came to me in prayer, a way of glimpsing what the crucifixion might have meant for all three persons of the Trinity. Take it as meditation, not theology. Why does God allow suffering? Obviously, that is a question I will not be able to answer but if you are suffering and going through a hard time it is easy to get mad at God and resent Him for letting you go through the suffering. You may think that God knows nothing of suffering, but I think this could not be further from the truth.

You can read history books and even read in the Bible to see terrible suffering and pain inflicted on people. Just in the book of Job alone, one could hardly imagine living his life. But even with all Job went through, I would say nothing comes close to what God Himself went through for us.

I am going to try to paint a picture for you of the day Jesus died on the cross for us. I am not going to go into the details of all the torture endured by Jesus by the Roman soldiers. There are movies you can watch and books you can read, but even without them, we all know it was excruciating for Him. We often fail to think about, however, is what that day was like for the Holy Trinity.

God had to sit and watch as His creation tortured and murdered His one and only Son. The Son who had been with Him since the beginning of time. The Son who had spent 33 years of His life being sinless and perfect and who did not deserve what was happening to Him. The Son whom God had watched over and listened to in prayer during those 33 years, all because His creation could not keep themselves from sinning.

It all started with Pilate feeling uneasy–a Roman who was probably numb to this type of violence, yet still knew that Jesus did not deserve the fate that was about to be handed to Him. Pilate tried to give Jesus a way out by asking Him, *"Are you the King of the Jews?"* (John 18:33 NIV)

I am sure Jesus, with His ultimate knowledge and wisdom, could have given Pilate many answers that might have set Him free. It almost seems as if this was a test—to see whether He would go through with accepting His role as the ultimate sacrifice for humanity's sin. Instead, Jesus answered,

"Is that your own idea, or did others talk to you about me?" (John 18:34)

This is the part where I can imagine things starting to get uncomfortable in Heaven. I can imagine the Holy Spirit coming to God asking, "Does He really need to go through this?" And God answering "There can be no forgiveness without the shedding of blood."

As the conversations between Pilate, Jesus, and the Jewish leaders continued to escalate, and as the torture of Jesus began, I imagine the angels in Heaven wanting to come down and put an end to Jesus's suffering, but not being able to do so.

Then God had to sit and watch as his son cried out and asked, *"My God, my God, why have you forsaken me?"* (Matthew 27:46 NIV), knowing there was nothing He could do, because there had to be a sacrifice for sin. Try to put yourself in that position for a moment and imagine the pain God must have felt. Imagine if that were your son. But that was not the end of it, for we must remember God is three in one. At the same time that God was mourning for his Son, He was not only feeling the emotional pain, but He was also feeling the physical pain, for He was actually on that cross at that same time. Now you have a God that for us, in one moment, is under immense physical pain and immense exhaustion, asking not to be forsaken and wondering if he must remain on the cross, but at the same time letting it happen, while feeling all the emotions of losing a Son. Both are going through the worst experience that can happen at the same time. This is unimaginable, isn't it? But there is still more. Now we have the Holy Spirit. Remember, three in one.

We now have the Holy Spirit in this moment having to sit back and watch two members of the Trinity going through unimaginable suffering, each hurting for themselves and each hurting for each other, with nothing any of them can do to help.

It is written in the Bible that for God, one second is like a thousand years, and a thousand years are but a second. In one moment, you have the Holy Trinity filled with unbearable sorrow, all three feeling what each other is feeling and none being able to help each other, all three feeling the physical and the emotional pain of the moment. I am sure for them every second of the crucifixion was like a thousand years, so it must have felt like thousands of years of suffering to allow us the grace to spend eternity in Heaven with them.

Let me just say, I am sure a lot of you found contradictions in what you just read. God, being omnipotent, does not second guess Himself. This was already prophesied earlier in the Bible, so God knew everything that was going to happen that day. But I just wanted to put out a different perspective of how truly difficult this experience must have been for the Holy Trinity and all of Heaven as well.

We so often think about this day as a day that God gave His only begotten Son to die on the cross for our sins, or the day Jesus sacrificed Himself for our sins so that the Holy Spirit could come to forgive sin and give us a new life. When we look at these things individually, it is easy to become overwhelmed and grateful for what They have done.

If we stop and think about this event as it played out for the Holy Trinity, the pain and emotions that were involved, we begin to realize the depth of God's love. We should thank the Holy Trinity every chance we get and be truly humbled and thankful for the gift we do not deserve. I just pray that God, being omnipotent, does not mean that He must relive that day over and over for us. I pray that that day was truly a single moment in history, because if it is not, the cost was truly too high for a sinner like me.

This image came to me while I was praying about a week and a half before Easter in 2024, and it really depressed me for some time. The images I saw during that prayer time were powerful, and it took me some time to get over them, if I even have yet. I think this really puts into perspective how much God really loves us. So the next time you are suffering and think God knows nothing of suffering, remember that He knows more than you could ever imagine. Following God is easy. All you have to do is give all areas of your life over to Him, trust in Him, and if we do this, we will have a peaceful, blessed life and live eternally in Heaven. But please don't forget what the cost of that was.

Reflection

Take a moment to truly thank God for all that He has done for you.

Six

What to Do if You Lose Contact with God

This could be the shortest chapter ever written in a book. If you have lost contact with God or feel your relationship with Him has faded, all you have to do is start praying. You can do it anywhere, at any time, and the more you do it, the stronger your relationship with Him will be.

But what do I pray about, or how do I pray? When Jesus was asked how to pray, He gave us the Lord's Prayer, which can be found in Matthew 6:9–13 and also in Luke 11:2–4. This is a good way to start your prayer, but if you do not know this prayer, you can just start talking to God and have a conversation like you do every day with anyone you encounter.

If you start your prayer and cannot think of anything to say, then you should count yourself very lucky, because this means you have no worries, no wants, and no problems. And if that is the case, you should thank God for everything that is going well in your life and all the things you have.

After you have let God know how grateful you are and still want to spend more time in prayer but are running out of words, you can ask the Holy Spirit to pray on your behalf. Romans 8:26 says, *"In the same way, the Spirit helps us in our weakness. We do not know what we ought to pray for, but the Spirit intercedes for God's people in accordance with the will of God."*

This is how easy God makes a relationship with Him. Even if you don't have words to pray, you can ask Him to pray for you, and He will.

So what does that look like? It may be just sitting there in silence, spending a peaceful time with God. It may be that the Holy Spirit starts putting words in your mind or on your heart. The words may make sense and be understandable, or they may not, but as it is happening you will start to feel at peace. It is not always about the words, but more about the time spent with the Holy Trinity.

The more time you spend in prayer with the Lord, the easier it gets. If you start a daily routine of doing this and for some reason you miss one day, you will be surprised at how much you missed that time with Him.

Your time with God, if repeated frequently, will become very precious to you, but more importantly, it is very precious to God.

Reflection

How much time do you currently spend a day with the Lord?
How much time would you like to spend with the Lord?

SEVEN

What Will Life with God Look Like?

Now that we are starting a new relationship or renewing our relationship with God, what does that look like? I wanted to include a chapter in this book to help arm you for what evil is going to do to try and stop you, because it will happen, and if you know what's going on, it may make it easier to recognize and know what to look for.

The first thing that is going to happen if you set aside time daily or weekly with God is something unexpected will almost always come up at the time you scheduled to spend with the Lord. It may be something that seems urgent at the time, or it may be something not urgent but just seems more fun or entertaining than spending time with God.

If you are serious about your time with God, this will happen only every once in a while at first, but then it will become more frequent until you realize that at the end of the week that you have not spent any time with the Lord at all. This is then going to make you anxious and feel guilty.

Please realize if you miss your time with God, He is not mad at you for it, and it is not a sin. This is just a trick from the evil one, who hopes that you will feel so guilty that you will stop scheduling time with God so you will not feel like you are letting Him down. Know that you are not letting God down. Because if you don't have time scheduled with God to miss, you will most likely not spend any time with Him at all.

Also realize the person most hurt by missing your time with the Holy Trinity is you. If you want to stop evil from doing this to you, then if you miss your scheduled time with God, make sure to set aside another time in that same day or week to spend with Him. If you always find time somehow— one way or another—to be with God, you will be surprised how the original time you scheduled will open back up, because now evil knows you cannot be kept away from God.

The second thing that is going to happen as you grow in your relationship with the Lord is that you're going to start feeling guilty about things you never even thought about before. Please realize that this is just another trick of evil. The sooner you start to realize that when you feel guilty about things while growing closer to God, much of the time it may be either evil or your own insecurities creeping in, the easier it will be to deal with.

It is not God who is disappointed in you, but more likely that you are being disappointed with yourself. I am not saying that God will not start putting things on your heart that will begin to make you a better person, because He will. What I am saying is that you should go back to God in prayer and ask if it is something that you really need to worry about.

The more time you spend with God, the easier it will become to discern between His voice, your voice, and evil's voice. This is not easy, and even when you think you have figured it out, you will probably be wrong again.

Evil is very tricky, and I may have just given it another way to trick you. Now that you have read the sentences above,

I am sure that you will do something you know is wrong, and that sentence above will come into your mind: "This is just my insecurity. God does not care. I can keep doing it."

It is not fair that evil can play on both sides of the coin, which makes it extremely difficult to know if it is truly right or wrong. Like I said, this part is not easy, and the only way to figure out what is right or wrong is to pray to God for help or find the answer in the Bible.

If something is wrong in the Bible, then it is wrong—there is no dispute. If something is good in the Bible, then it is good. If you get that gut feeling that something is wrong, it probably is, and if you can live without it, then do without it. If you think it is silly and just evil trying to mess with you, then take it to God in prayer and work through it with Him.

Each person's walk with the Lord will be different. Things that I may be able to do, you may not be able to do, and vice versa. God knows our limits and our temptations. For example, I may be able to have just one beer or glass of wine with dinner and not feel guilty about it, but God may be leading you away from it because sometime in the future you might not be able to stop at one. So God may be impressing it on your heart now so you never begin that habit. I am sorry to keep dragging out this point, but I just want you to use common sense when thinking about this topic.

I wish I could write out a list explaining how evil will try to make you feel guilty and when you should follow that guilt, but I can't. All I can ask is that you always take your guilt to the Lord and remember that evil will use guilt aggressively against you.

The third thing that is going to happen as you grow in the Lord and start learning all the tricks of evil is that your life is going to get better. Once you stop falling for all the tricks of evil and continue spending time with God and growing in the Lord, you will find that you are going to be happier, you are going to be more at peace, and you will notice that things will start going your way. If this is the case, then why would I need to put it in this chapter as something to watch out for or a trap from evil? Well, because it is.

When your life starts to become perfect and everything you ever dreamed of starts to happen, you may become less and less reliant on God. It becomes very easy to stop spending time with Him, or to stop listening for the bigger and better things God has in store for you, because you are so comfortable. This is where the relationship stops growing and becomes stale again.

Like I said earlier, evil wins no matter the outcome of the coin flip. If it can stop you from getting into a relationship with God to begin with, it wins. But once it can no longer do that because you already have a relationship with God, it will try to stop you from growing with God, or even better, stop you from bringing others to God so evil can win again.

Evil will be okay to let you live a happy, comfortable life with a lukewarm relationship with God, as long as you don't continue to grow or help others grow. It will also like the fact that it now has something to take away from you—and something it can use to stop you from growing with the Lord.

Now you must decide whether you are okay with letting evil win because you are not willing to step out of your comfort zone. I am not saying that your life will not still be great—it will probably be greater than if you stay comfortable and grow stale with God—but there will be some uncomfortable situations when you step out of your comfort zone for Him.

The fourth thing that is going to happen is just a continuation of the paragraph above. Once you get out of your comfort zone and start going from being on the defensive—where you are simply trying to figure out how to live your own life in Christ—to realizing that you should help as many people as possible live this wonderful life you have found, then evil will start attacking you again.

You may lose friends, family members, or personal time but make sure you do not lose your time with God. Because as long as you have that, you will be able to handle anything evil brings your way. This may sound scary, and I have to admit it is a concern of mine in writing this book, but I am not going to let it stop me. Because once you know there is a God that gave His only Son on the cross for you—and all He asks in return is that you follow Him and have a relationship with Him, and tell others the good news—then how can we do anything else? I hope this chapter helps prepare you for what may happen. I know it will not make it easier, but I hope it helps you understand why it is happening and recognize the tricks evil may use against you.

Sorry, I can't help myself, there is a fifth thing, and it may be the most important thing that will happen. You will live your life, die, and go to Heaven. You will stand before Jesus and hear, *"Well done, good and faithful servant."* (Matthew 25:21)

This is the goal and the only thing that matters. Fortunately, I do not think we ever get to stop telling people about the good news. I go to a church with a lot of people who are in the latter stages of life and they all still want to keep fighting evil and letting people know about God and every one of them is truly happy and you can see the blessing that God has given them. I do not think there will be any regrets in Heaven but if there are any it will be for the people you could not help get to Heaven. It will not be friendships or the people you upset trying to get them to Heaven, it will be regret for the ones we could have helped and did not.

Reflection

What stage of life are you in right now and what stage are you willing to get to?

EIGHT

My Will, God's Will, and Evil's Will

I n the previous chapter, we discussed thoughts that evil may put into your head to trick you or deceive you. Can evil get into our minds and put thoughts in our heads?

This is something that is hard to find a definite answer to in the Bible, so it is not something I would be able to answer with a simple yes or no. I would hope, for some of the thoughts that come into my mind, that evil can. I certainly hope that some of the doubts, fears, and the bad thoughts I sometimes have about other people are not truly coming from me. I do know that the Holy Trinity can speak to us and give us ideas, because that is the only way I could have written this book.

I think, rather than trying to give a definite answer to the question, it is more important to learn how to respond to the thoughts as they come into our minds. If you do not want to commit to the idea that evil is around us putting thoughts, worries, and doubts in our heads, then you must accept that these thoughts are our own. Either way, it does not matter how they got there—but it does matter that we treat them the same way and recognize that they are not from God.

That is why it is so important to read the New Testament and learn the teachings of Jesus. Once you know how He would respond in different situations, it becomes much easier to process the thoughts that enter your mind. This process takes practice, but if you work at it, you will notice how much easier it becomes to disregard negative or evil thoughts so that you can spend more time focusing on peaceful and positive ones.

Another trick that evil may use against us is repetitive thoughts. You may have had an incident happen to you, or you may be working on a project where you cannot find a solution. Either way, if you find yourself thinking about the same issue over and over again and cannot focus on anything else, take that issue to God and ask Him to help you resolve it.

This is especially important if these thoughts are keeping you from your prayer time or interrupting your prayers. These thoughts may be more difficult to recognize as evil because they may not feel negative or give you that uncomfortable gut feeling. Often, they may simply be something that needs to be taken care of.

But be careful not to let any thought consume you if it is not connected to your relationship with God. This can happen even with things as simple as planning a vacation. Planning a vacation can be exciting and fun, and it is easy to get caught up in planning every detail. But make sure you don't become so consumed by those thoughts that everything else gets pushed aside. Before you know it, three days may have gone by without spending time with God or your family because you were completely focused on planning the trip.

You may justify it by saying you are doing this for your family, so it must be okay. But once the vacation is planned and evil sees that your thoughts can be consumed by something, it may replace that thought with something else. It could be a rude coworker, a rude waitress, a friend who did not treat you the way you expected, or—more likely these days—a political debate.

Once evil realizes it can fixate your thoughts on things other than God, it may start doing this repeatedly. This can lead to anxiety and exhaustion. You need to learn how to let things go. The best way to do this is through prayer with the Holy Trinity. Learn to focus on the peaceful, comforting thoughts that come during your time with the Lord. The more you pray, the easier it will become to recognize these thoughts.

Once you can recognize them in prayer, you can start to bring that same mindset into your everyday life. When we begin paying attention to where our thoughts come from, it becomes easier to keep positive thoughts and quickly let go of negative ones.

While I am still not there yet, my hope is that if this practice is repeated often enough, negative thoughts may eventually stop entering your mind altogether. This would truly be a peaceful life. I know from my own time in prayer with the Lord that it is possible to let things go and find peace during the time you set aside with Him. My desire is to reach a point where every moment of the day feels like the time I spend with Him.

Reflection

Can you tell the difference between your will, God's will and evil's will?

NINE

God Made Me This Way

God made us in His image, but does God make people a certain way? It is obvious from the different physical builds of people that God gives everyone different attributes and gifts to use as we go through life. But does God give us our personalities, or do we create that ourselves from our experiences and our own free will?

I would say because of our free will, we have the ability to shape our own personalities and that we can change them at any time we choose. I think it is easy for people to say, "God made me this way. I am headstrong and stubborn because that is the way I was made. God gave me this addictive personality that makes stopping these actions impossible for me."

I do believe that God gave some people more courage to stand up to evil and others more wisdom to lead. But the reason I can conclude that personality, no matter where you fall on the spectrum, can be changed is that God gave us a book on how to live and act.

The Bible does not have chapters for different personalities, or for different races, or for people born at different times of the year. It has one main purpose: to love the Lord above all else and treat each other as you would want to be treated. The goal is the same for all, not just for some. So please don't believe that you were made a certain way and therefore get a pass to sin or act in ways that contradict what the Bible teaches. And do not believe that you cannot change your heart with the help of the Holy Spirit. One of the stories in the Bible is about a man originally named Saul, who later became known as Paul. This was a man whose purpose in life was to persecute Christians. A man who believed it was his life's purpose to try and stop the Christianity movement. He even believed he was called by God to do so.

Unlike us, Saul was at a disadvantage. He didn't have the New Testament to read and learn from the teaching of Jesus's love. If he had that it would have been simple for him to know that persecution of anyone is not acceptable to God. He would have learned from the New Testament how you treat the least of God's children is how you treat Jesus Himself. Fortunately for us, the one thing he did have was an encounter with Jesus. This would be an encounter that would change his life and the lives of many more. I don't get lost in the symbolism that Jesus literally took away Saul's sight to open his eyes to the wrong way of life he was living. Through Paul's teaching in the Bible, we can be taught that even the most hardened of hearts can be changed with the help of the Holy Spirit.

Please don't believe that God made you in any way that contradicts the teachings of the Bible. One of the biggest lessons of the Bible is that people can change. This doesn't mean change is easy, or that struggles disappear overnight.

Paul's transformation was dramatic, but most of us change gradually, through daily surrender. The point isn't that change should be instant—it's that change is possible, and we're not defined by our worst tendencies.

Reflection

What are some attributes you can change to grow your relationship with God?

Why Are There So Many Religions For Just One God?

If following God is so easy, then why are there so many denominations in the world? It could be part of the reason I am writing this book. Following God should be as easy as following the Bible, confessing that Jesus died for our sins, and spending as much time as possible in prayer. This is also likely a tool of evil that we must watch.

When dealing with people from different Christian denominations, try not to get hung up on the things you disagree about in the Bible. Instead, realize that we all love God and we are all striving for the same goal—to love God with our whole hearts and to spend eternity in Heaven.

I say this may be a tool of evil because imagine what would happen if all denominations stopped spending their time and effort trying to prove their points and beliefs about the Bible and instead worked together to disciple non-believers. Imagine if we all came together to stand against evil and call it out in a unified manner, rather than letting it confuse us about which denomination is right or wrong, thus turning people away from God.

If believers could come together to accept the good things from every denomination and let go of the things we disagree with—rather than arguing about them—then the believers of God could truly come together to transform this world.

That still did not answer the question of why there are so many denominations. I would say this again goes back to the gift of free will. Some people need very structured and and disciplined teaching to help them stay aligned with God's values. Others don't like being told what to do and prefer simply showing up and worshiping the Lord. Some people enjoy a full hour of praise and worship music, and others prefer just one song. So God has given us thousands of Christian denominations worldwide that we can choose from.

This means we have no excuse to say, "I do not fit in or agree with their practices." If one Christian denomination does not feel right to you, then there is likely another one around the corner that practices worship differently. So until you have explored the variety within Christianity, it is difficult to say Christianity itself is not for you.

If you are new to faith or do not currently have a church, I would encourage you to start with the closest nondenominational church near you. God has put you where you are for a reason, and that reason may be that the church around the corner is the best place to grow in your relationship with Him.

When looking for a church, make sure that it teaches from the Holy Bible as the foundation of its beliefs. If a church primarily teaches from books other than the Bible, you may want to consider finding another church to make sure that you are being taught the true Word of God. Some people have read the Holy Bible many times and still say they learn something new each time they read it. So, until you can recite every word of the Bible from memory—or fully understand every passage—why would you look for answers anywhere else when you know it is the Word of God?

The Bible is a living Bible that will continue to teach you about God every day you spend time reading it. It contains all the answers you need. There is no reason to search anywhere else for God's word.

You may also want to be cautious of churches that place restrictions on communion. Communion is taken in remembrance of Jesus's sacrifice on the cross. If you are saved, have confessed all your sins to God, and love Him, there is no reason you should not be able to take communion. If you personally do not feel ready or worthy to take communion, that is your decision. But that decision should be between you and God, not something a preacher should decide for you.

If you try the closest church and it is not a fit, that is okay. You will always have another church to try the next week. This can even be true after attending a church for many years if you begin to feel that you are no longer growing spiritually there. It is okay to explore other churches. Sometimes visiting other churches helps you realize that the church you started with is actually where you are meant to be. The important thing is to keep an open mind and not let one bad experience discourage you from going to church at all.

Evil will often make sure that something goes wrong. So pray and seek the direction God is guiding you to take. He may lead you to try again, or He may lead you to a different church. Try to remember God's will, my will, and evil's will when thinking about church. Because if you listen to evil's will, you may never find a church at all.

Reflection

Do you have a church family to help you grow your relationship with God and is it a healthy one?

ELEVEN

Religion Versus a Relationship

There are 613 commandments, or laws, in the Old Testament. As Christians, we are asked to attend Sunday school, Bible study, and church services, especially at Easter and Christmas. We need to spend time reading the Bible and studying the Word of God. We need to tithe and donate our time to helping others, being the hands and feet of God. We need to become disciples. We need to worship God. At the beginning of the year, we have the 40 days of Lent which begin on Ash Wednesday and end after Holy Week. Holy Week begins with Palm Sunday, Holy Monday, Holy

Tuesday, Holy Wednesday, Maundy Thursday, Good Friday, and Holy Saturday, then Easter Sunday. We have All Saints' Day, and then we enter Advent to start the Christmas season four Sundays before Christmas, followed by Christmas.

When you put it all together, it can start to become too much and may seem overwhelming, but I would like to caution you that everything above is part of religion, and none of it will get you into Heaven by itself. What gets you into Heaven is a relationship with God the Son, God the Father, and God the Holy Spirit.

We need to remember that all the things above are meant to grow your relationship with God and bring you closer to Him. None of them are requirements for salvation, and if you are just doing them to make God happy but are not spending any actual time with God or growing in a relationship with Him, then you have missed the mark.

Jesus talks a lot about the religious leaders of His day. They followed every letter of the law but did not truly know God. And they often prioritized some laws over others. If you read Matthew 23, there are many verses that are "woes" to the teachers of the law and the Pharisees. He calls them hypocrites and tells the people to do everything they tell you to do, but not imitate them, because they do not practice what they preach. The Pharisees Jesus talked about cared more about religion and doing the actions required by the religion than using those practices to learn about and spend time with God.

There is also Mark 2:27, in which Jesus said, *"The Sabbath was made for man, not man for the Sabbath."* Now, please don't get me wrong, or think that I am saying you do not need to involve yourself in any of the things mentioned in the first paragraph in this chapter. That is not at all what I am saying.

What I am saying is that if you are going to do any of them, do them to glorify God. Do them to grow your relationship with Him. Don't just read the Bible to check it off your list. Read it to fully experience the WORD of God and try to be present in that moment with Him.

Don't just go through the motions during Holy Week. Truly praise "Hosanna" on Palm Sunday and mean it. Truly thank Jesus for dying on the cross for your sins.

Don't just show up to church and go through the motions. If you do, the only thing you get out of that is feeling better about yourself, but this does not grow your relationship with God, and that is the purpose of going to church.

This is also true with tithing. Do it only if you truly believe that everything you have is a gift from God and want to show Him that He is truly first in your life. Give because you believe He will do far more with that money to grow His kingdom than you ever could. Do not do it just because you are supposed to, or in hopes that He will give you more if you give more to Him. This may be the outcome you get, but do not do it for that reason.

Tithing is one of the areas in the Bible where we are invited to test God. Malachi 3:10 says, *"Bring the whole tithe into the storehouse, that there may be food in my house. Test me in this,"* says the LORD Almighty, *"and see if I will not throw open the floodgates of Heaven and pour out so much blessing that there will not be room enough to store it."* While this could be a great result of tithing, this is not the reason to tithe.

The main point of all this is to be careful not to make religion your god. Religious practice exists to help us grow in our relationship with God. Making a list of items and checking them off one by one accomplishes nothing if you do not do them truly for God or to grow closer to Him.

Following the 613 laws is great practice and will help you live a better life, but if you are doing them just because you were told you are supposed to, and not learning why God wants you to follow them in the first place by being in a relationship with Him, then the gain you get from doing them will be nothing.

I also think that all the practices in the first paragraph of this chapter will not become overwhelming if you do every one of them while you are truly doing them with and for God. It is important at first to choose the ones that bring the most growth to your relationship with God.

Reflection

What are the things you love to do for the Lord, and what are the things you feel you have to do? Do they help you grow your relationship?

____

____

____

____

____

____

____

____

____

____

____

____

TWELVE

I Pray But Hear Nothing

Earlier in the book, in the chapter "What to Do if You Lost Contact with God," we talked about how to pray if you never have, or if it has been a while since you have prayed. But I would like to go over prayer time for believers who spend lots of time in prayer but feel they are not receiving the answers they need.

It has been a few weeks since God has given me any new material for this book. Granted, I have been letting life and worldly things get in the way and not spending as much time and dedication as I should for someone who believes he was given direction from God. I started to let the thoughts of the enemy take over, and I began thinking that I did not put forth the effort that was required for this task, so maybe God has moved on and found others to do the job He gave me. Lately, I have been seeing lots of new works and teachings coming out, and many of them seem to cover the same areas as this book I am writing—but from much more learned men and women than me.

When I first started this book, I would sit down, spend time in prayer, and ask the Holy Spirit what I needed to write about that day, and it was easy. Ideas would fill my head. Sometimes there were so many ideas that it was hard to keep them all in my mind. It was so nice spending that time with Him that I did not want to stop praying, but I would have to so I could get the ideas that were given to me written down.

But for the last two weeks, when I prayed, nothing was coming to me. And at this point, the book is way too short to publish. Right now, it would just be a pamphlet, not a book. But I am not one who is going to give up. I know I would regret it for the rest of my life if I did not complete this task.

So, I started praying again the same way I had been for the past two weeks. I was still not getting direction on anything. At this point, I had to plead with the Holy Spirit to let me know how long I was going to have to pray before I started getting direction or ideas again. I asked the question, and I waited.

But this time, as I waited, I noticed that I started thinking about chores that needed to be done. Then I started thinking about relationships that I needed to pray about and people that I needed to pray for. I do this all the time when I pray, because praying is spending time with God and letting Him know everything about you. This type of prayer is great for spending time with God, but not great for getting answers from Him.

The more and more I sat there, the more thoughts and distractions kept coming into my mind. It then became easy to realize what was happening. The Holy Spirit hadn't gone silent. I had stopped listening. My mind was so full of my own concerns that there was no room left for His voice. If you need an answer to a prayer and are not getting it, maybe it is because you are not taking the time to listen to the answer.

It would have been nice if it had not taken me two weeks to learn this lesson. But most of Jesus's teachings in the Bible are given through parables, probably because you learn the lesson better when you come to the answer on your own. The one thing I can learn from this is that if I had stopped asking the question, I would never have found the answer. That is why I will keep repeating in this book the importance of maintaining that relationship and spending time with God.

Reflection

When was the last time you heard from the Lord, and how long has it been?

THIRTEEN

Teach Me How to Teach Others

A disciple is one who accepts and assists in the spreading of the good news of Jesus Christ. To do this, we must be able to share this good news with non-believers, or else we are just preaching to the choir. I think this is a concept that is hard to grasp, and sometimes, as Christians, we may get it wrong.

As you start to grow in your faith and learn how to discern between the different voices you hear, you may find yourself not wanting to willingly take part in some of those activities you once enjoyed or spend time with people you once enjoyed.

If you go to church regularly, you will probably even hear some sermons about being careful about who you spend your time with. You may hear the phrase, *"Do not be unequally yoked."* This comes from (2 Corinthians 6:14 ESV). This verse tells us not to be involved with unequal partners or not to partner with non-believers. This is truly great advice if we are talking about business or marriage, but I think sometimes Christians try to use this verse to avoid associating with any nonbelievers. If we do this, then how can we call ourselves disciples? I think it is even more important to be around nonbelievers, so that we can show them how wonderful life can be when you are dedicated to following Christ.

The difficult part is making sure we present ourselves in a manner that represents Christ well. This can be challenging to learn, and at times it may feel overwhelming. It may start to feel like, as Christians, we can never have any fun, or that we will be judged.

This is where you must have a strong relationship with God and feel secure in your walk with Him. Only God can judge you, and your relationship with Him is ultimately between you and Him. If you cannot be around certain people because it will cause you to slip in your relationship with God, then do not spend time around them until you grow strong enough to do so. But once you grow stronger, I would encourage you to go back to them to show them how much happier you are. This may be the only chance they will have to see the love of Christ in their lives—and it may come through someone they know.

This is not just for friends and family. It applies to all the people you interact with in your day-to-day life. I am not asking you to go get in someone's face and preach the gospel to everyone. That would probably turn more people away than it would bring to Christ.

What I am encouraging you to do is read the teachings of Jesus and live your life the way He would. When you do this, you may find that it brings peace to your life. Others will see that peace, and some of them will want it. When they want it, they may come and ask you questions about the peace you have.

If someone else starts the conversation, they will often be more receptive to the answers than if the conversation is forced upon them. Living without constant worries, fears, doubts, or anxiety about life is something everyone desires, but few people ever truly find. I believe it would be fair to say that many non-believers may never even have the opportunity to experience this, because there is no way to fully find this peace without God.

The main point of this chapter is simply to live your life in a way that makes people curious enough to come to you and ask about what you have. There will still be times when we need to initiate the conversation. The Holy Spirit may bring people into your life whom He wants you to approach and begin a conversation with, because some people will never ask the question unless someone first brings it up.

When this happens, try to be polite and do more listening than talking at first. The Holy Spirit may prompt you what to say, but it may still be difficult not to become emotional and use your own words and ideas.

It is natural to feel excited when sharing the good news, but we must remember that we are there to answer their questions, not to push our agenda. Sometimes you may need to take a moment to assess how the conversation is going.

If you encounter someone who becomes angry as soon as you begin speaking, and insists that there is no God, you might ask them why they feel such anger toward God. They may explain why they feel that way, and that may open a door for conversation. They may say they are not angry with God because they believe there is no God, but that they simply dislike people pushing religion on them. You could ask them how often this really happens to them. The likelihood is that it does not happen very often. If they acknowledge that, you might then ask again why the topic creates such a strong emotional reaction.

To me, it is illogical for people to hate something so strongly if they truly believe it does not exist. For example, if someone told you they had an imaginary friend named Johnny and that they talked to Johnny all the time, most people would not feel anger toward Johnny. They might just think the person was mistaken or imagining things. But they would not have an emotional reaction toward Johnny.

Yet many people have strong emotional reactions toward God while claiming He is not real. You might invite them to reflect honestly on what is causing that anger. Sometimes, deep down, people struggle with God because they sense that He is real.

Again, the most important thing you can do is remain polite, listen carefully, and allow the Holy Spirit to guide your words. If they decide they no longer want to continue the conversation, that is okay. You may have planted the seed they needed in order to start seeking God. And sometimes planting the seed is all we are called to do. Just as no one can come between your relationship with God, you cannot force your way into someone else's relationship with Him. That part is between them and God.

Reflection

Am I ready to be a disciple? If not, what is holding me back?

FOURTEEN

Randomly Opening the Bible to Hear from God

For some reason, I have been having an extremely hard time writing this chapter. The order of the chapters in this book is not the order in which they were written. Many of the chapter titles were put in place for me to come back to later.

This was a chapter that was placed on my heart to write, but every time I tried to write it, something would stop me or something would come up. I began to wonder if it did not belong, and I almost took it out. But as I was removing the title, something called me back to put it in again, so hopefully this works, and it is a chapter you will get something out of.

Believe it or not, there is a word for randomly opening the Bible to receive an answer. It's called bibliomancy. I would encourage you to seek your answer through prayer first. God can use many avenues to answer prayers, and the Bible is definitely the number one place to go.

But we still need to go back to the ideas of "my will, God's will, and evil's will" when choosing such randomness in answers to a prayer—especially if you are doing this for life-changing decisions.

First, if you apply the "my will" to bibliomancy, you most likely have a desired outcome to the question you are asking. If that is the case, you may not interpret the verse the way God intended you to. Instead, you may conform the verse to your own will in order to get the answer you want.

Like I said before, I hope evil does not have enough influence over us that it could point us to a Bible verse that would mislead us from God's will. But on the chance that it does, you still need to take the verse back to God to make sure it truly came from Him. If anything does not seem right, or it is confusing as to what the answer from the verse might be then I would hold off on saying that you found your answer.

If you try bibliomancy and the verse seems perfectly suited to answer the question you were asking, then it may be God's will. But even if it feels perfect, it would still not hurt to take it back to God in prayer.

You may also want to research the verse further. Unless you have gone through seminary, most of us will still need some context to understand what a verse is truly about. Go back to the beginning of the book and read the entire passage. Find out who the author was and why he wrote the book. God may be trying to show you more than you were originally looking for.

There are rarely shortcuts in life, and spending more time in the Bible is never a bad thing.

One thing we can say for sure is that God will never tell you to do something that contradicts the Bible. There is a joke often told about bibliomancy. It is a story about a man who wanted to find out what plans God had for his life. So he closed his eyes, opened the Bible randomly, and placed his finger on the page. When he opened his eyes, he read Matthew 27:5, *"Judas... went away and hanged himself."* Not liking that answer, the man tried again. This time, his finger landed on

Luke 10:37, *"Go and do likewise."* Again, not liking that answer, the man tried once more. This time, his finger landed on John 13:27, *"What you are about to do, do quickly."* While this may be a joke, it still illustrates why our answers need to come from a relationship with God.

If you have daily or weekly time that you spend reading the Bible or praying, I do not think you will need to rely on bibliomancy. The answers you seek will be revealed during your normal time with God. And if the answer is not revealed right away, it may simply be that you are just not ready yet, or that it is not time for you to receive the answer. God has far more patience than we do, but the answer is always better when it comes at God's perfect time.

Reflection

What is the number one source you use to get answers from God?

FIFTEEN

How to Pray for Healing

I must be honest, when I was praying and the Holy Spirit put this chapter on my heart, I was a little reluctant. He was also putting the chapter about using the Bible to hear from God on my heart, and I would much rather write that chapter right now than this one.

I do not see myself as very competent to write about this. I have family and friends that I have been praying for, and they are still not healed. So how can I tell you how to pray for healing if I have never healed anyone myself, and not everyone I pray for is healed? There are, of course, some people that I have prayed for who have been healed. So why some and not others?

I can only write what has been placed on my heart and what I have learned over the years. And again, there are going to be lots of contradictions that evil may try to use in this area of prayer. That is the reason it must be in this book. I cannot just continue writing things that are within my comfort range, like in the previous chapters.

Some will say if your faith is strong enough, you will only need to pray once. If the prayer is answered, then it is God's will, and if not, then that is also God's will. Once you ask, then God knows your request, and you should not have to keep bothering Him with it.

Others believe in persistent prayers—praying so much and so often that God gets tired of hearing you and answers your prayer. So which one is right?

I would say they are both right. God wants a relationship with you, so, we should be careful with both approaches. Just asking once and believing that it is a bother to ask again is not a healthy relationship with the Lord. You should always feel comfortable coming back to God with your concerns. And if your prayer was not answered, I think it is perfectly okay to ask why and begin searching your heart for understanding.

On the other hand, when praying persistent prayer, be careful that is not the only time you spend with God. You need to ask yourself if you are truly in a relationship with Him, or if all your prayers are about your own needs and wants.

Also, be mindful that if your persistent prayer is answered, that your prayer time does not suddenly disappear. I am not saying that God would allow pain in your life because it is the only way you spend time with Him. But the relationship with God is more important than the pain itself. And I believe that the more peaceful time we spend with God, the easier all situations in life become.

Once you put all your worries and cares in God's hands and accept the outcome, the stress of life begins to fade, and you can focus again on living with peace.

There are other things the Bible tells us to consider when praying for healing. First, do not carry hate toward any of your fellow people. It is hard to forgive yourself and accept healing if you cannot forgive others and hold hatred in your heart. This teaching appears immediately after the Lord's Prayer—the prayer that Jesus taught us to pray. (Matthew 6:14-15 ESV) says:

"For if you forgive others their trespasses, your Heavenly Father will also forgive you, but if you do not forgive others their trespasses, neither will your Father forgive your trespasses."

Second, you need to believe that what you are asking for is possible. If that is difficult for you, then ask the Holy Spirit for help. Ask Him to strengthen your faith and your relationship with God until you reach a point where you trust completely that you and God are aligned.

Third, be willing to accept the healing. Sometimes, people who have been in pain for a long time start to accept that pain as their normal reality. As weird as it may seem, some people may even feel afraid of living without pain. It can become easy to say no to things when you have an excuse and that excuse can slowly become a crutch if you let it. If God is willing to heal you, do not be afraid to accept the healing and start enjoying life again.

Another way to pray is to begin your prayer by thanking God for the healing you are about to receive. Say, "God thank you for healing me," even before you are healed. Start out praying with faith so strong that you believe your prayer will be answered, and do not let go of that faith. The stronger your relationship with God becomes, the stronger your faith will grow. After all, how much easier is it to ask something from your family and close friends than it is to ask a stranger?

Never forget that God does all things for a reason. Even if we do not understand those reasons, we can still find peace by turning the situation over to Him.

Reflection

What type of prayer do you use for healing—one-time prayer or persistent prayer? Does it ever vary on a case-by-case basis? If so, why?

Sixteen

Faith

D oes it take more faith to calm the storm, or more faith to sit in the middle of the storm as if it's not even there? In (Mark 4:35-41 ESV) it says:

On that day, when evening had come, He said to them, "Let us go across to the other side." And leaving the crowd, they took Him with them in the boat, just as He was. And other boats were with Him. And a great windstorm arose, and the waves were breaking into the boat, so that the boat was already filling. But

He was in the stern, asleep on the cushion. And they woke Him and said to Him, "Teacher, do you not care that we are perishing?" And He awoke and rebuked the wind and said to the sea, "Peace! Be still!" And the wind ceased, and there was a great calm. He said to them, "Why are you so afraid? Have you still no faith?" And they were filled with great fear and said to one another, "Who then is this, that even the wind and the sea obey Him?"

Should the disciples have had the faith to calm the storm themselves? Or should they have just let Jesus sleep and had the faith to ride out the storm as if it were not even there? Maybe they did exactly what they were supposed to do. They called out to their Lord and Savior to help them.

If you notice, Jesus asked the question, "Have you still no faith?" But He never received an answer. Above is how the chapter ends, and Mark 5 begins with them already across the lake. This just shows that Jesus doesn't need to know why you lacked faith in the past, as long as you find it in the future. He will always be there.

What is Faith? It is everything! It is what it takes to be a follower of God. You can never have that relationship with God if you do not believe He is real. You will never make the time or the effort if you don't fully believe. Ask yourself now, where is my faith today? Matthew 17:20–21 tells us that if you have faith the size of a mustard seed you can tell mountains to move, and they will. Nothing will be impossible for you.

Now we just need to figure out what kind of faith we have. When you asked yourself where your faith is today, What was your answer? Was it simply, "Yes, I believe," and that was it? Or was it an overwhelming feeling that came over you—one that made you want to put the book down and thank God for His grace and mercy?

I think the question of where our faith is may be the most important question we can ask ourselves, and it is one we should ask often. Faith is not religion. Faith is a relationship. Faith is the loving connection we were created for. We were made in the image of God, and our faith is the only way we can bring peace to our souls.

But we still have not answered the question. Does it take more faith to calm the storm, or more faith to sit in the middle of the storm as if it were not even there? I have not answered it because the answer is for you to decide, and it may be different in every situation.

We know our faith will be tested, the Bible tells us this. You must decide whether you need the faith to calm the storm yourself, because we have been granted that power through the Holy Spirit. Or you may choose to sit, wait, and remain faithful, knowing that God will always take care of you. You may also run to Jesus and say, "Lord, please help me." If you do none of these things, you can be assured that the boat will sink.

Following God is easy. All you have to do is give every area of your life over to Him and trust in Him. When we do this, we will have a peaceful blessed life and one day live forever in Heaven. (1 Peter 1:8-9 ESV) *Though you have not seen Him, you love Him; and even though you do not see Him now, you believe in Him and are filled with an inexpressible and glorious joy, for you are receiving the end result of your faith, the salvation of your souls.*

Reflection

Where is my faith at this point in my life?

Seventeen

Live Your Best Life

What is living your best life? Social media would have us believe that it is constant adventures and parties all the time—vacations, social gatherings, dinners, lunches, breakfasts, and endless time with family and friends. We only have so many days on earth, so we should live every one to the fullest. But is this what God put us on this earth to do? I would have to say yes—absolutely live every day to the fullest and enjoy life. I am sure that is not what you were expecting me to say when you first read the question, but I do believe that God genuinely wants us to live wonderful, fulfilled lives.

He even gave us a book that tells us how to do it. It is the Bible. The Bible gives countless testimonies about the lives of many people, and we should use these testimonies to understand how to live our own lives. As you read them, there is one overwhelming recurring theme: Those who put God first and dedicated their lives to Him lived full lives and often experienced better outcomes than the ones who turned their backs on God.

In the Old Testament, we are given a lineage of many kings. As you read through it, we see a pattern: this king was good and followed God's ways, then another king was wicked and turned his back on God. There are forty-two kings and one queen mentioned in the Bible. Did all their stories make it into the Bible so we could have a complete lineage of the Jewish people? As I write this chapter and the Holy Spirit leads my thoughts, I feel like it may have been more than just to give us a history lesson. In the preface, I began this book by saying, "Following God is easy. All you have to do is give all areas of your life over to Him and trust in Him, and if we do this, we will have a peaceful, blessed life and live eternally in Heaven." I then followed that statement with, "Wouldn't it be nice if it were that easy? If we could just read the sentence above and our brains would instantly accept it." But we know it is not that simple. The lesson needs to be repeated and reinforced. So perhaps God gave us forty-three examples—forty-three stories—to help make sure we understand. These stories remind us that while life will not be perfect just because we follow God, it will be far better for us—and for people around us—than if we choose to ignore Him.

So if we are all here to live our best lives, does that mean we should quit work and just party all the time? Obviously not. One of the main ideas I want emphasize throughout this book is common sense. Many times, the evil one tries to convince us to ignore our common sense. We all know someone who tries to live their "best life" by partying constantly. And while they may appear to be having fun in the moment, we can often see that they are not truly happy, and eventually their life begins to spiral out of control.

What about people who do not struggle with substance abuse? If you won the lottery tomorrow and never had to work again, what would you do? Would you go on endless vacations and buy beautiful houses with housekeepers and private cooks? That may sound like a great life, but material possessions and shallow relationships will never bring true peace and happiness. The only way to experience true inner peace—peace without any fear or constant worry—is to place your hopes and dreams in God. When you believe God will take care of you no matter what happens, and that your relationship with Him will always remain as long as you continue to seek Him, you begin to experience a peace that the world cannot offer. This is the only true peace you will find in this world.

Material possessions can always be taken away, and any personal relationship you form on this earth can fade away or be removed from your life. The only thing in this world that can stay consistent and bring you total peace every day of your life is a relationship with God the Father, God the Son, and God the Holy Spirit. No one and nothing can keep you away from that if you desire it, and the more you engage in it, the more you will desire it.

Now you may tell yourself, "I can go on a hike, climb a mountain, fish, meditate, or spend a relaxing afternoon with my family." We all have different things we enjoy that can bring us temporary peace. These things are great, and as much peace as they bring you, I can tell you that if you include God in them, you will enjoy them even more. I also believe you will find yourself doing them more often, because you enjoy them so much more.

That would be the first step: discover how much more enjoyable things in your life are with God. The second step would be to bring God into all the things you do not find enjoyable. If you do not find work enjoyable, and you catch yourself wishing you were somewhere else, take a break and spend a few minutes with the Holy Trinity, and watch how much your mood improves. If there is a problem you are having at work, ask God for help and see how easily you find a solution to your problem.

If it is a really bad day—for example, you are in a major accident or one of your friends or family members is—then you don't need to read this book for me to tell you to pray, because that is usually the time we all do. But the point is don't make that the only time you pray. Instead, already be in good standing with the Lord. His will may be done either way, but you will be more accepting of the outcome and be more at peace with it if you already know how to lean on the Lord and already have that relationship with Him. While we know not every day will be wonderful, we can still be at peace during the bad days if we have that relationship with God.

So now we are spending time with God on the best days of our lives and the worst days of our lives, so what is next? Start spending the other days in between with God. Every day, do more things with the Lord and include Him in your daily life until you find that He is present in everything you do. If you do this, I believe you will find you are truly at peace and living your best possible life. I would challenge you to tell me a way to live in this world by following worldly ways without God in your life. You may be able to live a good life, but you will never live in total peace, because there will always be fear of something, or there will be conflict or loss, and in those times you will have no one to turn to. I know this may seem like a lot of time and effort, but if you do it and find peace, it will be well worth it. If you do it and do not find peace, then the only thing you will have lost is the time you invested. And what is time on earth without God? We were made in the image of God and created to be with Him, and because we were made to be with Him, we will never truly be happy or find lasting peace apart from God.

Reflection

How would a greater relationship with God help you live your best life?

Eighteen

Life without God

If God is not real, then what is the purpose of life? The only purpose of life, if there is no God, is to reproduce in order to keep humanity in existence. Once you have reproduced and raised your offspring so they can reproduce more humans, then what else would you have to offer? Life truly has no meaning without God. Without the gift of eternity, if we are only here for one hundred years and then gone forever, what does it matter what we do? What does it matter what our ancestors did, or what future generations will do, if eventually the sun burns out or a comet hits the earth and extinguishes all life?

That is why I know there is God, because I believe we can all feel that there is more to this life than just reproducing. Now take some time to ponder this dilemma. Try to find a purpose for life without God. Does it matter what the 117 billion people who came before us did, or what the 117 billion people who may come after us will do, if there is no eternity in Heaven to follow? For me, the answer is no. I do not believe there is any true purpose to life without God, and I want my life to have purpose. So now that I desire purpose, the only purpose that remains for me is to get myself, my friends, my family, and everyone else who will listen to me to Heaven. Then, when I have spent one hundred years on earth and enter Heaven, I can hear, "Well done, good and faithful servant," and I will know my life had a purpose. If I spend the rest of my life doing this and my life eventually comes to an end and there is no God, then at least I will have lived a peaceful life without fear. I will still have no regrets and will end up the same as the 117 billion people who came before me. But if I did not do this—if I did not try my best to help myself, my friends, my family, and others find their way to Heaven—then not only would my life feel wasted, but the risk of eternity in hell would be far too high a cost to ignore. So, to me, there is no downside to living every day with God. And once you decide to take that step, and once you decide to give your life peace and purpose, why not be fully committed if you have a God who desires to have a relationship with you for eternity.

Our lives with God are like getting into an airplane. While we are in that plane, we are safe and can rest. But if you were to jump out of that plane, it may feel exciting at first. It may even feel like you are flying. But what is actually happening is that you are falling. And the farther you get from the plane, the more fear will begin to grow. The more the anxiety will begin to take hold. Soon, you will be so focused on the ground that you will not even look back at the plane. Eventually, you may wish you had never left that plane. And if you do not find a way to get back to it, you will never feel that safety again. Finally, all that will be left is the ground rushing up to meet you.

We are one created being—mind, body, spirit, and soul—all in one. But our soul is the part of us that was created to be with God, and will never be at rest without Him.

Reflection

Could you find a true purpose in life if there were no God and no eternity?

____

____

____

____

____

____

____

____

____

____

____

____

____

Nineteen

Living the Perfect Life

Living the perfect life is probably not possible. Even in the Bible, God lets us know that not every day is going to be perfect. He also tells us that, as believers, we will have troubles in our lives. So then why write a chapter that might seem to give false hope?

I think the purpose of this chapter is to consider how we might make this imperfect life we have feel more like a perfect one. Let us imagine what our lives would have looked like if we had never been removed from Eden. In that world, we could go to God with all our questions. We would not have any fear, worry, or doubt because we would know that God would always take care of our every need. We would not be jealous, envious, or insecure. There would be no reason to hate your fellow man, woman, or child because the things that they do would be between them and God and would not change our relationship with Him. In Eden, the only concern would be how our relationship was with God. We would rely on God for every aspect of our lives without question and know that all our needs would be met. That sounds like a wonderful life, doesn't it? That sounds like a perfect life.

Unfortunately, we are no longer in Eden. We must work and labor to make a living, but do we have to fear? Do we have to worry and have doubts? Do we have to be jealous, envious, or insecure with the lives we have been given? I hope by now, at this part of the book, you already know the answer to that question. Following God is easy, so why do we make it so hard? We are not in Eden, but we can go to God with all our questions. We can give all our fear, worry, and doubt to Him. We can choose not to worry about anything other than our relationship with God. Following God is easy, so why do we make it so hard? It will take time to give every moment of every day to God. I can say it. I can write it. But I am nowhere close to being able to do this yet, and I do not know why. It should be easy, but I can tell you the more you do it, the easier it gets. Just remember the next time you get frustrated or need help that following God is easy, so why am I making it so hard? If it helps, you can also ask yourself: Will I care about this situation in a million years? Will I care about this moment one year from now? If the answer is no, then you should not be so concerned about it in the moment you are in. Just give it to God and be at peace. This truly is how easy God has made life for us. Now it is just up to us to have faith and live it out.

Reflection

What can I give to God to make my life easier?

TWENTY

Putting It All together

I pray and hope that while you were reading this book you received inspiration or found ways to grow your relationship with the Lord. There were a few instances in this book where I tried to stay humble and let you know my true feelings and thoughts as I was writing. In the first chapter, I started out by saying, "As a person, I am not qualified to write this book, but as a vessel for the Holy Spirit, we are all qualified to do all things through Christ." There were two chapters where I let you know that I was having trouble writing. I hope that did not cause the message of those chapters to be questioned.

I did it to show you that I had to rely on faith and not my own understanding of the topic. Hopefully, seeing that process in the pages of those chapters will help you move forward the next time you need to rely on faith. We are all given gifts from the Holy Spirit, but only through prayer and relationship with God will we find out what they are. I pray I used mine to help you grow your relationship with God.

I also wanted to let you know that we all have the same access to God. The religious leaders of this world do not have any more access and are not loved more by God than you are. They may have more faith and a better relationship with God than we do, but they do not have more access or love. No one on this earth can do anything through Christ that you cannot do if you have a strong relationship with God.

Following God is easy. All you have to do is give all areas of your life over to Him, trust in Him, and if we do this, we will have a peaceful, blessed life and live eternally in Heaven.

Wouldn't it be nice if it were that easy? If we could just read the sentence above and our brains fully accept it? Instantly, we could give all our fears, cares, worries, and anxiety to Him and feel everlasting peace.

Well, I hope now when you read that statement, you have some tools and an understanding of just how easy it can be if we do not make it complicated. You now have the tool of letting go of any contradictions that hold you back. You know that because of eternity, God does have time for you. You now know how to pray to distinguish His will, your will, and evil's will. You know that you can change to be more like Jesus. You know that there are thousands of denominations within Christianity, and you just have to find the one that helps you grow with God, while at the same time learning that the relationship with God is far more important than the religion. You know that faith, above all, is the essential foundation of your relationship with God, and that prayer can bring an answer to all your questions. But sometimes, to hear the answers to our prayers, we must be still and simply listen. You now know that you are a created being, created to be with God, and without Him, you will never be fulfilled or truly at peace in your life. Now that you know all these things, please do your part and let others know the good news. You also know that no one can come between your relationship with God. But the most important thing to take away from this book—the one point that has been repeated more than any other—is the relationship. The relationship is more important to God than anything else, and that is the easy thing we can do. That is why following God is easy.

Reflection

Following God is easy. What am I doing that makes it hard?

Closing

I would like to end this book with a prayer for all the readers. "God, please bless the readers of this book and bring your Holy Spirit upon them to show them how much you genuinely love them. Let them know that while life will not always be easy, if they have You in their life, it will be easier. God, please let today be the beginning of a greater relationship between you and the readers of this book. Help them grow stronger in their faith and their love for you. It is in Jesus's name I pray. Amen."

About the Author

Vern Kaska is a Colorado-based Christian author and Voice and Network Engineer who has designed global networks across more than fifteen countries. Though not formally trained in theology, Vern writes from a place of daily prayer, Scripture study, and a deep personal relationship with Jesus Christ. His passion is Christian living, spiritual growth, and helping readers build a stronger relationship with God. Inspired by faith and real-life experience, Vern's mission is simple: to reach hearts worldwide with the life-changing truth that following God is easier and more powerful than we think.